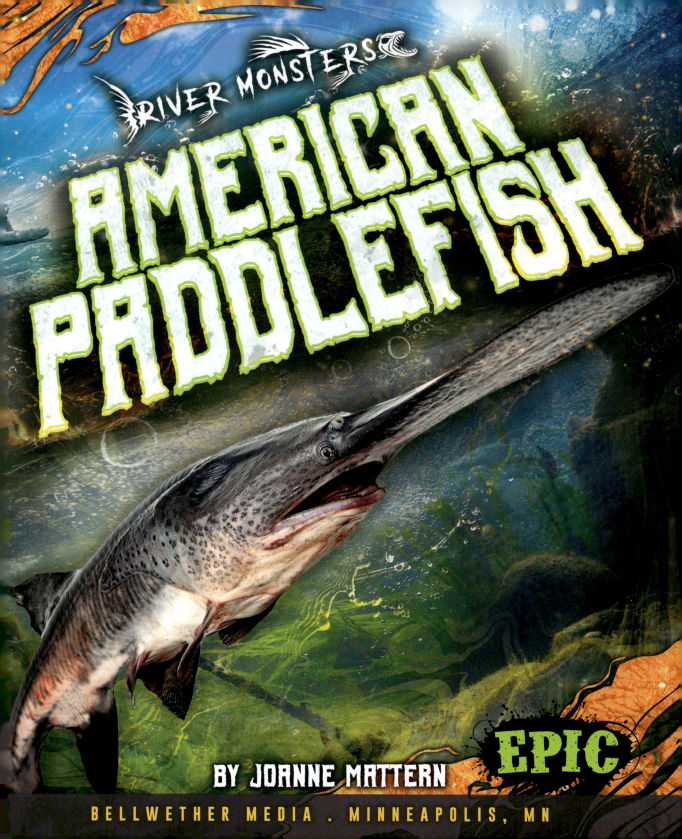

RIVER MONSTERS

# AMERICAN PADDLEFISH

BY JOANNE MATTERN

EPIC

BELLWETHER MEDIA . MINNEAPOLIS, MN

# EPIC

This edition first published in 2024 by Bellwether Media, Inc.

Library of Congress Cataloging-in-Publication Data

Names: Mattern, Joanne, 1963- author.
Title: American paddlefish / by Joanne Mattern.
Description: Minneapolis, MN : Bellwether Media, 2024. | Series: Epic: River Monsters | Includes bibliographical references and index. | Audience: Ages 7-12 | Audience: Grades 2-3 | Summary: "Engaging images accompany information about American paddlefish. The combination of high- interest subject matter and light text is intended for students in grades 2 through 7"-- Provided by publisher.
Identifiers: LCCN 2023039901 (print) | LCCN 2023039902 (ebook) | ISBN 9798886878356 (library binding) | ISBN 9798886879292 (ebook)
Subjects: LCSH: Paddlefish--United States--Juvenile literature.
Classification: LCC QL638.P755 M38 2024 (print) | LCC QL638.P755 (ebook) | DDC 597.42--dc23/eng/20230901
LC record available at https://lccn.loc.gov/2023039901
LC ebook record available at https://lccn.loc.gov/2023039902

Editor: Elizabeth Neuenfeldt    Designer: Josh Brink

Printed in the United States of America, North Mankato, MN.

# TABLE OF CONTENTS

# HEY, BIG SNOUT!

American paddlefish are known for their unusual **snouts**. They look like paddles!

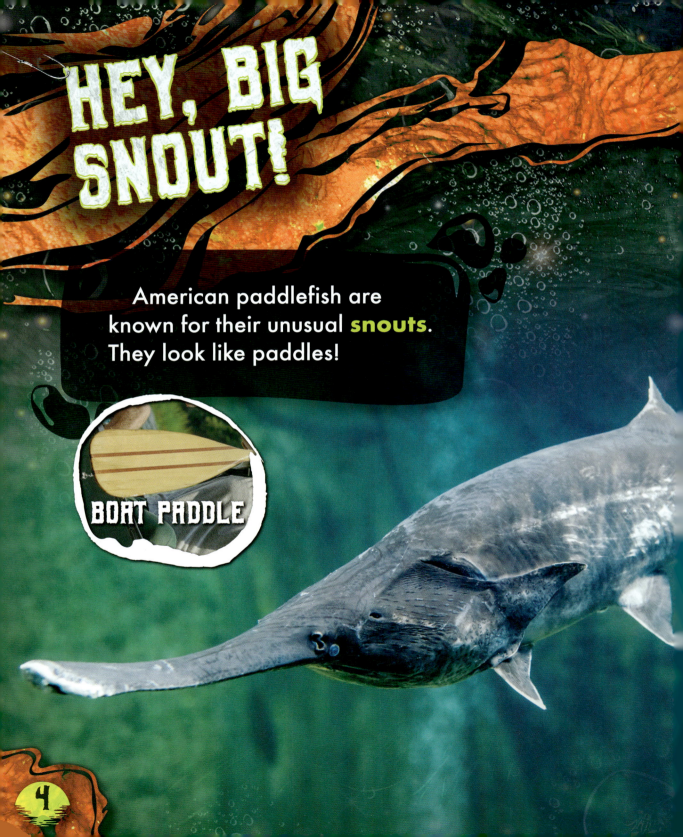

BOAT PADDLE

These fish are from the United States. They live in the Mississippi River. They also live in nearby lakes and rivers.

# AMERICAN PADDLEFISH RANGE

RANGE =

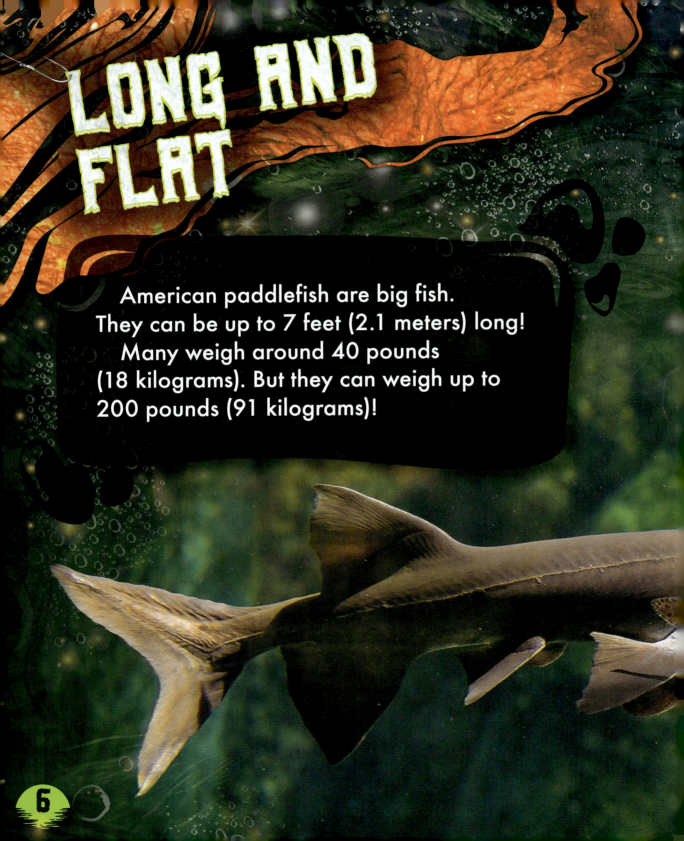

# LONG AND FLAT

American paddlefish are big fish. They can be up to 7 feet (2.1 meters) long! Many weigh around 40 pounds (18 kilograms). But they can weigh up to 200 pounds (91 kilograms)!

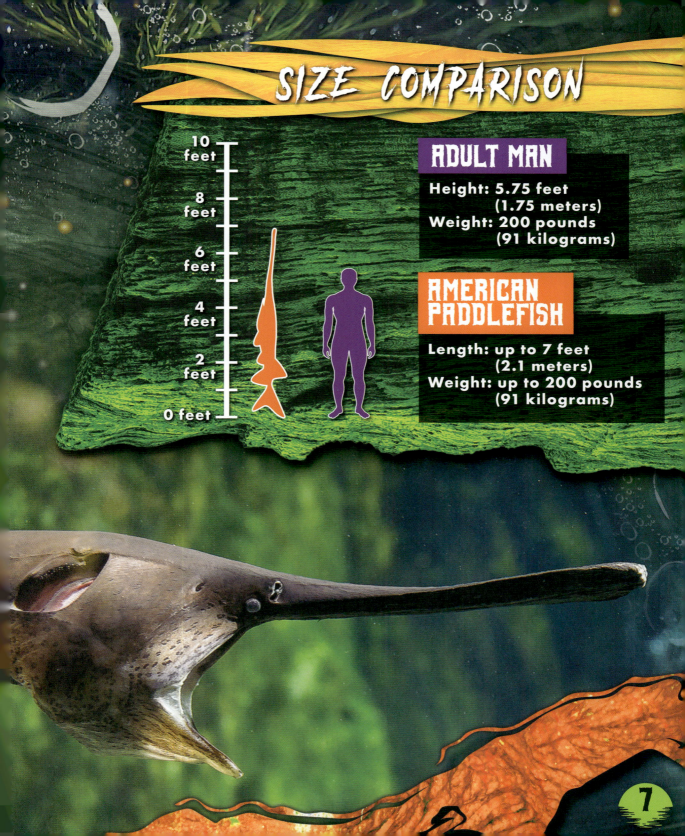

# SIZE COMPARISON

10 feet
8 feet
6 feet
4 feet
2 feet
0 feet

## ADULT MAN

Height: 5.75 feet
(1.75 meters)
Weight: 200 pounds
(91 kilograms)

## AMERICAN PADDLEFISH

Length: up to 7 feet
(2.1 meters)
Weight: up to 200 pounds
(91 kilograms)

Paddlefish have very few bones. These fish are mostly made of **cartilage**.

They have almost no **scales**.
Their skin is very smooth.
They are mostly green or gray.
Their color helps them hide in water!

## PADDLEFISH OR SHARK?

Paddlefish and some sharks look alike! Both animals are mostly made of cartilage. But they are not closely related.

These fish have small eyes.
Unlike many fish, their eyes
look down. They cannot see well.

## FROM LONG AGO

Paddlefish are the oldest
kind of animal still alive in
North America. They may
have been alive before
dinosaurs were around!

They have **taste buds** on the bottom of their long, flat snouts. These help paddlefish find food!

These fish have large mouths.
They do not have teeth. They are
**filter feeders**.
They also have big **gills**.
These help them breathe underwater.

GILLS

# IDENTIFY AN AMERICAN PADDLEFISH

**LONG SNOUT**

**SMOOTH SKIN**

**SMALL EYES**

**LARGE MOUTH**

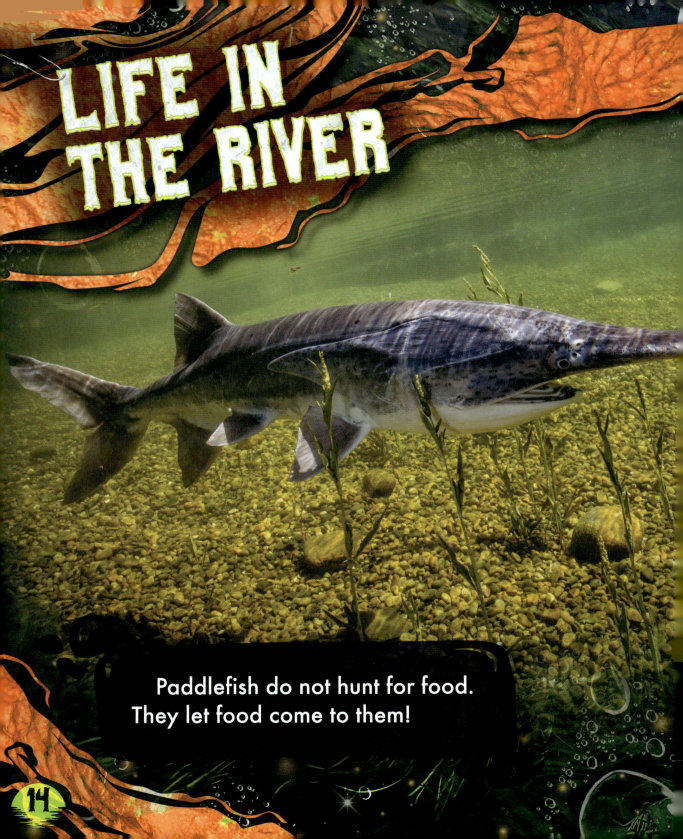

# LIFE IN THE RIVER

Paddlefish do not hunt for food. They let food come to them!

They swim with their mouths open. Their mouths fill with tiny plants and animals called **plankton**.

In the spring, adults swim up rivers.
They **spawn** on gravel bars.
The eggs hatch about a week later.
The young fish grow up on their own.

# RECORD CATCH

**WEIGHT**
164 pounds
(74 kilograms)

**LENGTH**
Unknown

**WHEN WAS IT CAUGHT?**
June 22, 2021

**WHERE WAS IT CAUGHT?**
Keystone Lake, Oklahoma

YOUNG AMERICAN PADDLEFISH

# PADDLEFISH IN DANGER

American paddlefish are a **vulnerable species**. They are losing their **habitats**. Dams and **levees** block them from swimming upstream. They cannot spawn.

**Overfishing** has also put these fish in danger. People hunt their eggs and eat them.

# ONE OF A KIND

Chinese paddlefish once swam in China's Yangtze River. But they died out in the 2000s. Today, American paddlefish are the only living kind of paddlefish.

**AMERICAN PADDLEFISH EGGS**

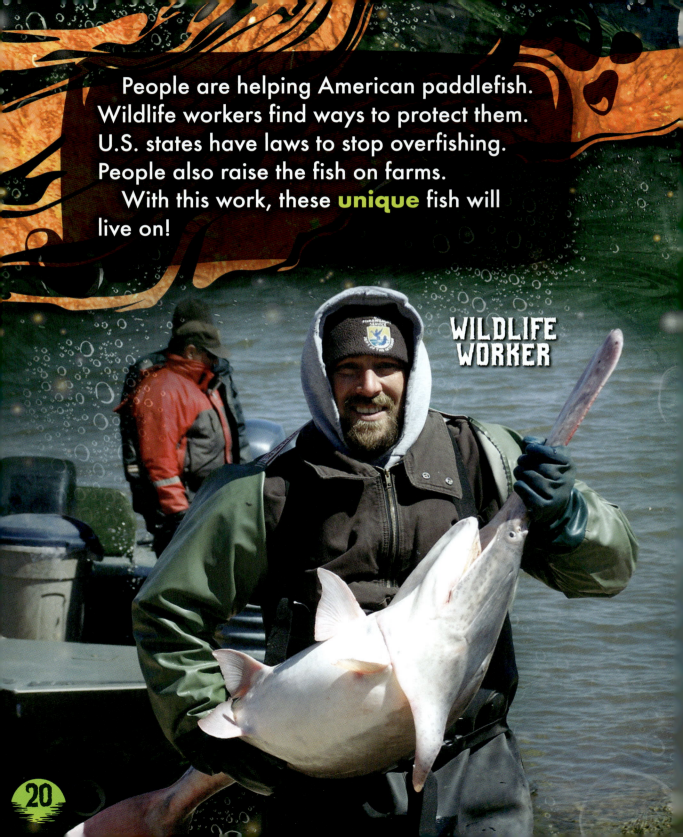

People are helping American paddlefish. Wildlife workers find ways to protect them. U.S. states have laws to stop overfishing. People also raise the fish on farms.

With this work, these **unique** fish will live on!

WILDLIFE WORKER

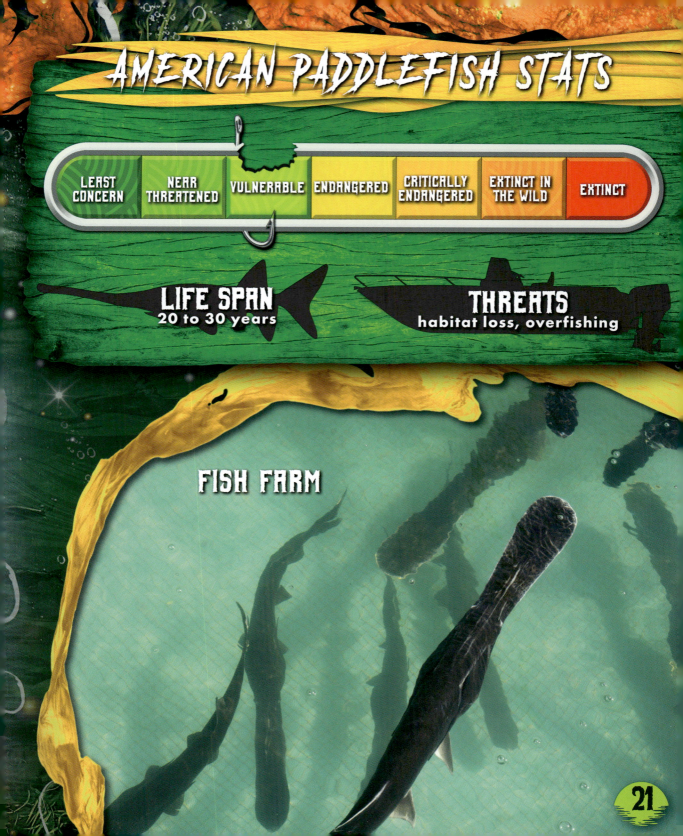

# AMERICAN PADDLEFISH STATS

| LEAST CONCERN | NEAR THREATENED | VULNERABLE | ENDANGERED | CRITICALLY ENDANGERED | EXTINCT IN THE WILD | EXTINCT |

**LIFE SPAN**
20 to 30 years

**THREATS**
habitat loss, overfishing

FISH FARM

# GLOSSARY

**cartilage**—a strong, light material that makes up some animal skeletons instead of bone

**filter feeders**—animals that get food by filtering nutrients and tiny living things from the water

**gills**—parts along the sides of some animals that help them breathe underwater

**habitats**—places where animals live

**levees**—banks built along rivers to control flooding

**overfishing**—using up the number of fish by fishing too much

**plankton**—tiny plants and animals that live in water

**scales**—small plates that cover the bodies of some fish

**snouts**—the noses and mouths of some animals

**spawn**—to lay eggs

**taste buds**—tiny parts that help sense food

**unique**—one of a kind

**vulnerable species**—animals at risk of becoming endangered

# TO LEARN MORE

## AT THE LIBRARY

Green, Sara. *Rivers*. Minneapolis, Minn.: Bellwether Media, 2022.

Jacobson, Bray. *The Mississippi River*. New York, N.Y.: Gareth Stevens Publishing, 2023.

Mattern, Joanne. *Alligator Gars*. Minneapolis, Minn.: Bellwether Media, 2024.

## ON THE WEB

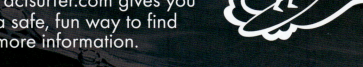

FACTSURFER

Factsurfer.com gives you a safe, fun way to find more information.

1. Go to www.factsurfer.com.

2. Enter "American paddlefish" into the search box and click 🔍.

3. Select your book cover to see a list of related content.

23

# INDEX